Table of contents

I see

I see.

I see a pig.

I see a hen.

I see a bird.

I see a cow.

I see a horse.

I see a duck.

I see a dog.

Words:

I, a, see.

Punctuation:

(.)

Sounds:

/s/ /th/

I see the

I see the dog.

I see the rooster.

I see the hen.

I see the sheep.

I see the goat.

I see the cat.

I see the duck.

I see the rabbit.

Words :

I, the, see.

Punctuation:

(.)

Sounds:

/s/ /th/

The farm

A farm.

I see a farmer.

I see the farm.

A tractor.

I see the tractor.

The scarecrow.

I see the scarecrow.

The farm.

Words :

a, I, the, see

Punctuation:

(.)

Sounds:

/s/ /th/

We see the farm

We see.

We see a tractor.

We see the hay.

I see the wheelbarrow.

We see a shovel.

We see a fence.

I see the field.

We see the corn.

Words :

a, I, the, see, we

Punctuation:

(.)

Sounds:

/s/ /th/

We can see the farm

I can.

I can see.

We can.

We can see a scarecrow.

We can see the seeds

I can see the cows.

We see a cat.

I can see the can.

Words :

a, I, see, the, we

Punctuation:

(.)

Sounds:

/s/ /th/

Made in the USA
Las Vegas, NV
09 November 2024

11009687R00033